Music Minus One Vocals

2127

COME FLY WITH ME

Big Band Arrangements

Music Minus One Vocals

COME FLY WITH ME

CONTENTS

ISBN 978-1-941566-27-5

There'll Be Some Changes Made

from ALL THAT JAZZ

Words by Billy Higgins
Music by W. Benton Overstreet

5

God Bless The Child

from BUBBLING BROWN SUGAR

Words and Music by
Arthur Herzog Jr. and Billie Holiday

How High The Moon

from TWO FOR THE SHOW

Lyrics by Nancy Hamilton
Music by Morgan Lewis

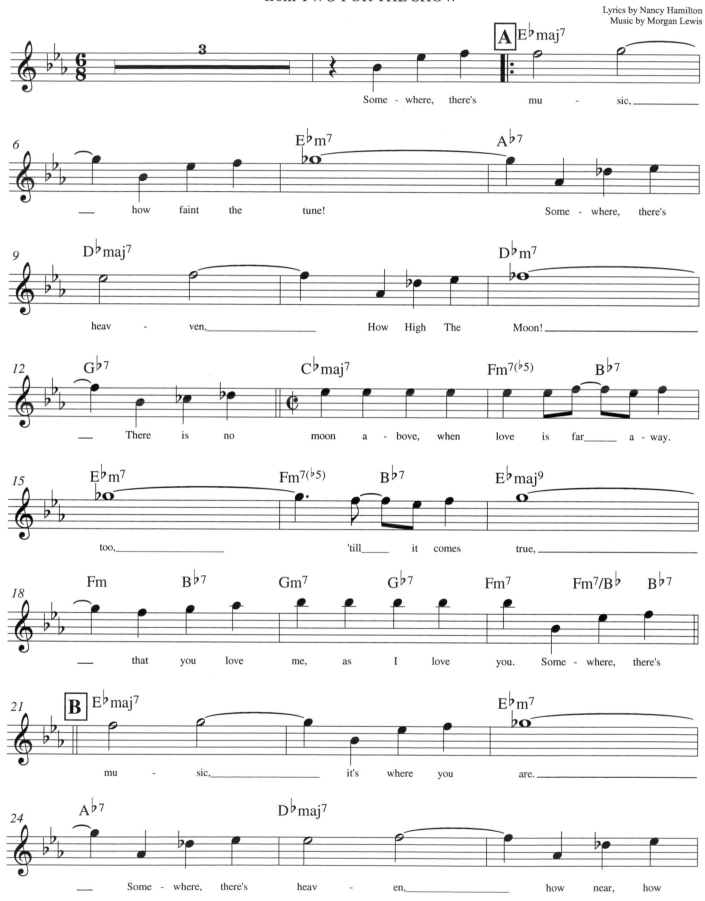

10

MMO 2127

This page left blank to facilitate page turns.

Why Don't You Do Right

Music and Lyrics by
Joe McCoy

13

MMO 2127

Come Fly With Me

Words by Sammy Cahn
Music by James Van Heusen

15

MMO 2127

This page left blank to facilitate page turns.

I Apologize

Words and Music by
Al Hoffman, Al Goodhart and Ed Nelson

Volare

Music by Domenico Modugno
English Lyric by Mitchell Parish
Original Italian Text by Domenico Modugno
and Francesco Migliacci

*Come on girls, we're going to do the Volare,
a la macarena! Here we go!*

oh, oh, oh, oh. No

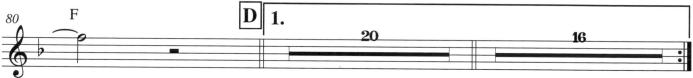

wond - er my hap - py heart sings, Your love has giv - en me wings.

Nel blu di - pin - to di blu,

Fe - li - ce di sta - re las - su

Nel blu di - pin - to di blu,

Fe - li - ce di sta - re las - su

Oh, Vo - la - re!

The Candy Man

Music and Lyrics by
Leslie Bricusse / Anthony Newley

The Way She Makes Me Feel

Music by Michel Legrand
Lyrics by Alan & Marilyn Bergman

Music Minus One
50 Executive Boulevard • Elmsford, New York 10523-1325
914-592-1188 • e-mail: info@musicminusone.com
www.musicminusone.com

MMO 2127

ISBN 978-1-941566-27-5